SATURDAY NIGHT IN YORK STREET

20/6/82

Pearl,

many thanks for your
interest in 'Saturday night in
York St., I hope you enjoy
reading about the old district
and the old days.

Best Wishes

John Campbell

SATURDAY NIGHT IN YORK STREET

John Campbell

illustrated by
Hector McDonnell

The
Blackstaff
Press

British Library Cataloguing in Publication Data

Campbell, John
 Saturday night in York Street.
 I. Title
 821'914   PR6053.A/

 ISBN 0–85640–267–2

© John Campbell, 1982

Published by The Blackstaff Press Limited
3 Galway Park, Dundonald, BT16 0AN

Printed in Northern Ireland by
Belfast Litho Printers Limited

Contents

The Place

'Sailorstown, is this it?' said the young
  boy to his dad.
'Stretching all around you,' said the father
  to his lad.
'It's the greatest district. Finer people
  you won't meet.'
'Ack Da,' said the wee buck,
  'All I see's a dirty street.'

Saturday night in York Street

The smell of pigs' feet boiling, with nabs and ribs and noints,
Greeted all the men-folk as they rolled home from the joints.
Mother cut the soup-greens whilst waiting for her sire,
Then bathed the children briskly in a tub beside the fire.
That was Saturday night in York Street; boyhood memories
    remain. . .
Saturday night in York Street will never come again!

When Dad rolled up the hall, half drunk, you'd ask him for a 'wing',
Of course you wouldn't get it, until he'd heard you sing.
He'd sit amongst his cronies, and make 'em all keep hush,
Whilst you stood there knees a'trembling and warbled like a thrush.
That was Saturday night in York Street; Papa liked an old refrain. . .
Saturday night in York Street will never come again!

You'd get to pour some Guinness, and help hand round the soup,
Whilst songs were sang impromptu by the happy friendly group.
Your mum and dad would giggle as you hid behind the sink,
Pretending not to notice when you stole a little drink.
That was Saturday night in York Street; empty bottles you would
    drain. . .
Saturday night in York Street will never come again!

Being carried up to bed by a rather shaky dad,
Who tucked you in with tenderness, for he loved his little lad.
He'd let the mantle flicker, 'cause he knew you loved to hear
The melodies that drifted from the voices sweet and clear.
Saturday night in York Street brings a tear I can't contain. . .
Saturday night in York Street will never come again.

Sailorstown

In Sailorstown was some good men,
   and many a punch-up we had then,
But we'd all finish friends again
    . . . in Sailorstown.

In Sailorstown the drink was good,
   and many men used it for food;
It put them in the fightin' mood
    . . . in Sailorstown.

In Sailorstown no copper's nark
   dared to walk if it was dark –
They didn't cotton to that lark
    . . . in Sailorstown.

In Sailorstown the streets were small;
   not much space from wall to wall;
Each room no bigger than a horse's stall
    . . . in Sailorstown.

In Sailorstown each little street
   boasted women, clean and neat.
The kitchen houses looked a treat
    . . . in Sailorstown.

In Sailorstown nobody moaned,
   although the streets were cobblestoned.
Friendship – that was all they owned
    . . . in Sailorstown.

In Sailorstown they 'waked' their dead,
   and smiled when two young ones were wed;
At births they 'wet the baby's head'
    . . . in Sailorstown.

In Sailorstown a motorway
    sprawls where once tough men held sway,
Where happy children used to play
    . . . in Sailorstown.

In Sailorstown was some good men,
    I wish I was back there again.
No finer souls I've met since then
    . . . in Sailorstown.

45 Earl Street

I took a walk down Earl Street, maimed and blinded Earl Street,
I took a walk down Earl Street and cried just like a child.
The street was foul and sated, the houses corrugated:
Blinded, gagged, deflated amid the rubble piled.
Some were gashed already, and stood alone, unsteady,
Somehow proud and ready. . . yet frightened all the while.

I found the house that reared me. . . appearancewise it scared me.
I spoke. . . I'm sure it heard me as I walked its saddened hall.
It creaked a muted greeting, like gurgled water leaking.
I thought I heard it speaking, saying, 'Welcome, Welcome Home'.
I saw the room I'd slept in, and very often wept in,
When love was unrequited and days were sad and long.

The staircase bore me gladly, my heart was beating madly.
I viewed the bedroom sadly where my parents used to sleep.
Sunlight had streamed 'round it, before the wreckers found it
And manacled and bound it with concrete blocks and brick.

As I stood there time went flying, and I heard my mother crying;
In the parlour saw Dad lying in a coffin brown and gold.
I turned quite resolutely, the house observed me mutely.
I studied it astutely, and I'm sure I saw it smile.
So I walked out into Earl Street, maimed and blinded Earl Street.
I stood awhile in Earl Street, and cried just like a child.

The Sportsman's Arms

Just opposite Brougham Street it sits in a nook,
Where York Street lies sprawled like an unfinished book,
The years have swum by it, but now it's no more.
The thread has been spun, Barnie's closin' the door.

He sold damn good likker to Jim, Jack or Joe.
It was commonly known that he hadn't a foe.
He also sold Heaven to heads that were sore,
But the deed has been done, Barnie's closin' the door.

We had some good times in that beat-up old boozer.
He'd give you some heart if you'd backed the last loser,
Then slip you a stake to get goin' once more.
But that's all behind us, he's closin' the door.

The guys that he's leavin' are soon gonna know,
We won't meet his equal wherever we go.
Professional down to his soft-hearted core:
    An era has ended.
        He's closin' the door.

Drinking in a pal's house

Some get drunk to bawl and shout, but we get drunk to spout about
the times we had when grass was green. Before this hard life turned
us mean. And made us seldom drop our guard, except with pals all
drinkin' hard. Then coats come off and sleeves get rolled, and
stubborn bottle-necks get holed.

The drink flows brown or white or black, and eager hands reach for
their 'whack', and soon the worldly mask slips down, and scarce a
face contains a frown. And some voice edged with laughter's ring
begins a pleasant song to sing!

And someone says, 'Remember when we took on Billy Fisher's men.
In spite of being under odds, we whipped 'em cold with fists and
clogs. By God, this whiskey's sharp and sweet. How can you
drink that Vodka neat? Are you still chasing Maggie Sparks or
have you found another mark? You lucky dog, you got the looks –
the only ones I get are kooks, but kooks or not they're all the same
– Contenders for the marriage game.'

'Hey Tommy, tip that bottle some. I've reached the dregs of this yer
rum. Man, it's a pity this must end, and we must take the
homeward bend, to bed and bear dull life again. . . I tell you pal it's
not the same, an hour spent here with all you guys. . . is Heaven in
this fellow's eyes.'

Song of a ship

When the fog lies low on the harbour, and the Quays are bare and
   bleak,
It's then I find on the waterfront, the solitude I seek.
The giant, sleek ocean-going 'Ladies' overshadow me as I walk.
Oh, the tales they could tell of distant lands, if only they could talk.

Some have been stripped of their cargoes, and lie with their bowels
   bare.
Others are deep in the water, carrying more than their share.
Footsteps ring as an alien walks some deserted deck.
Perhaps he's dreaming of his own shores, and wishing he was back.

It's early, and the sleeping ships are beautiful in repose.
Somewhere beyond my vision, a mournful foghorn blows.
Those restless ships don't like it, being tied by head and heel.
They'd rather race unbridled, with the master at the wheel.
With screeching growls, she'll weigh the rusty anchor to her side,
And roll to sea from the shabby Quay, on the breast of the morning
   tide!

York Street

I'd just got off the Heysham boat, I landed with a frown.
I looked around the place I loved, the place called 'Sailorstown'!
I was very disappointed when nobody hove in view
And I began to wonder if the song they sang was true!

> *No matter where ye roam me lad,*
> *No matter where ye flit,*
> *In India, Timbuctoo, Russia or Tibet,*
> *America, Australia, China or Japan,*
> *No matter where ye roam me lad,*
> *You'll find a York Street man.*

Just then a fella came in view, he looked me in the face.
Says he, 'Ye're Billy Murpie's son, I'd know ye any place.
I'm glad to see ya home again, and lookin' in the pink.
C'mon across to Eugene's and we'll have a little drink.'

> *'Cause no matter where ye roam. . .*

Says he, 'I'm thinkin' 'bout the time, way back in Forty-Two.
In France the bombs were fallin' fast, as thick as Irish Stew.
We charged with bayonets flailing, and cut the Gerries down
'Cause half of our platoon was born and reared in Sailorstown.'

> *'Cause no matter where ye roam. . .*

They say when Edmund Hillary conquered Everest,
He sat down rather heavily, his strength sapped by the test.
The Abominable Snowman around an ice-ridge ran,
Retreating from a fist-fight with a burly York Street man.

> *'Cause no matter where ye roam. . .*

Now Churchill in his memoirs, he mused an awful lot,
About a place in Belfast, it's a tidy little spot.
He said, 'If someone peeves you, and for war you've got a yen,
Never try to win it without some York Street men.'

> *'Cause no matter where ye roam. . .*

9

The Devil he came up from Hell, he had a look around,
Hoping he could find some toughs, to take back underground.
He got them from the Shankill, the Falls and Sandy Row.
But down along old York Street, he was afraid to go.

 'Cause no matter where ye roam...

The People

'Buck Alec', Rinty Monaghan,
James Galway, Gerry Fitt,
All are first-class York Street men
with talent, strength and grit.

The York Street Flute

There's never bin a band like the York Street Flute,
Be it brass band or silver, cavalry or foot.
From Rangoon to Rathcoole, from Russia to Kilroot,
There's never bin a band like the York Street Flute.

They blow up the Shankill, they blow up Sandy Row,
They'd blow up the Falls, but the cops won't let them go.
They'll blow till they're purple, steppin' out in style.
If ya wash 'em down with whiskey, man they'll walk a million miles.
There's never bin a band like the York Street Flute. . .

Dempsey played the lead drum, a man of high renown —
He's known in every village, every hamlet, every town;
Some say he's sixty, while others say he ain't,
But we're all aware his favourite words is 'pint, pint, pint'.
There's never bin a band like the York Street Flute. . .

They walked with the Seaver Lodge, one morning in July;
They went to the Master's house, and drank the poor man dry,
But when they strode along the road, they played as smooth as silk
Although they'd drunk most everything except the baby's milk.
There's never bin a band like the York Street Flute. . .

The last time I saw 'em, they walked into Lewis Street,
Blew out and spewed out, they could hardly stand their feet.
The cops who were with them tried to lend a hand,
By becoming dummy fluters with the York Street Band.
There's never bin a band like the York Street Flute. . .

Whenever there was trouble, they always got the blame.
They changed their name a hundred times, but still remain the same.
Dempsey's gone but they still plod on, each year they
     walk the route,
But no matter what they call themselves, they're still the
     York Street Flute
There's never bin a band like the York Street Flute. . .

Suckered

I was standin' in Barnie's, just havin' a beer,
  and thinkin' the thoughts of the poor.
After boozin' all night I just didn't feel right.
  I was glad I'd enough for a cure.
That's when the bar-room door opened
  and somebody shouted 'Repent.
If you don't seek salvation, this good day,
  to the bowels of Hell you'll be sent!'

His voice pierced its way through my eardrums,
  and kicked at the pain in my head.
If my poor shattered brain had been clearer,
  I'd have finished the likker and fled.
His gimlet eye fixed on my features,
  his grimy hand clutched at my coat.
'A rich man will not enter Heaven;
  them's the truest words ever bin spoke.'

He roared this out as he grasped me,
  an' glared at the drink in my hand.
'The money that bought that,' he uttered,
  'could have bought food for some dyin' man.'
Now normally, I'm not a sucker
  for guys with the gift of the gab,
But this one had nettled my conscience,
  with his wild and yet accurate stab.

The rain drizzled off the bar windows,
  the sky seemed so dull and so dark.
If I gave him dough, then I'd just have to go.
  And wander alone in the park.
But somehow this thought didn't hurt me
  as much as the look in his eye.
So I fished my few bob from my pocket
  and reached it to him with a sigh.

15

He vanished within a few seconds,
   I wearily finished my drink,
And walked through the snug to the bar-door,
   and what I saw there made me blink.
My 'religious' friend sat quite contented,
   a whiskey and pint at his side.
'What's this?' I managed to utter.
   'Can't go out. I'd be drenched,' he replied.

Kings for a day!

Kings for a day – I know 'em well – get their pay, then run like hell.
Off to the nearest bookie's or bar; to toss it away, like a Hollywood
    star.

Before even washing the grime from their faces, they're off to indulge
    in the daily horse-races.
From bookie's to bar-room, with money they'll sprint, and throb
    with excitement – until they get skint.

'Beat in a photo' or 'Fell at the first', they'll tell you with venom,
    whilst slaking their thirst.
Gone to the bookie's, each penny they got – except for a pint or two
    saved from the pot.

Suddenly dawns that the wife's dough is blown; now desperation
    and panic is sown.
But a loan these days is easily found. If they don't mind paying five
    bob to the pound,
The 'Shark' will add them to his round. If they miss a week, he'll hunt
    them down.
Search for work the whole week through. If there's no work. what
    can they do?
They've got to keep the 'Shark' up too; they've got to pay the interest
    due.

Thursday comes. . . they get their pay. Off like bullets, right away.
Never learn. Never care. From pub to bookie, like a mad March
    hare.
Grimy faces, bright yet grey. . . 'Gimme a pint. . . I'm King for a day!'

Skint again

Skint again; no lesson learned.
  Fingers ache from being burned.
Good advice it's all bin spurned,
  'cause I'll be back again tomorrow.
Work real hard to get a stake;
  sling cement without a break.
Seems it's all for the bookie's sake;
  'cause I get left with only sorrow.

Wife gets mad, it's not her fault;
  I'm just too stubborn to call a halt.
Defeat is sour – it tastes of salt;
  aw well, there's a 'spell' to borrow.
Broke again, it's a bitter pill,
  seems I'll never 'ring the till'.
Somehow I know I never will,
  but that don't stop me tryin'.

Losers – Losers – makes you sick;
  wonder why your head's so thick.
Crawl away, your wounds to lick;
  you'll try again, tomorrow.
Wife needs money, food is dear;
  rent needs payin'; kids need gear.
You'll bring it home, she needn't fear;
  until you reach the bookie's.

Get too old to sling cement;
  health and money's all bin spent.
Chasin' horses the Devil sent!
  Aw well, roll on the pension!

A jug of Barnie's wine

The fight was goin' bad for Jim; he'd hit the canvas twice.
And Kelly's left was cuttin' him as if it were a knife.
But Big Jim turned the tables with a punch that was divine,
When his 'second' soaked his gumshield in a jug of Barnie's wine.

It cud fly aeroplanes or fuel trains or juice a shipside crane.
It banished ills, done away with pills and made redundant pain.

Wee Tammy couldn't get a girl because he was quite small.
He'd chat 'em up quite bravely, but they'd never, never fall.
But now he knocks 'em sideways lookin' down from six-foot-nine.
Since his mama washed his stockings in a jug of Barnie's wine.

It cud fly aeroplanes or fuel trains or juice a shipside crane.
It banished ills, done away with pills and made redundant pain.

Bob Johnston had a stammer, it made his life a hell
When he began a story it would take a day to tell.
But now at Queen's he lectures in a voice that's sure and fine,
Since his grannie soaked his dentures in a jug of Barnie's wine.

It cud fly aeroplanes or fuel trains or juice a shipside crane.
It banished ills, done away with pills and made redundant pain.

It clears the grit from binmen's throats.
It helps the dockers empty boats.
It makes the sailors feel quite gay.
And sends the carters on their way.
And underneath each coat you'll find,
The magic known as Barnie's wine!

Kiddo

They called him Kiddo in boyhood days, it stayed with him through
    life.
Grew up tough, though grey as granite, still was Kiddo to his wife,
Features marked from endless fighting, brain perhaps a trifle shook,
Slow to rile, but devil-wild, possessor of a mean right hook.

Kiddo was, for all his toughness, friendly as a little lad.
His bullet-head was often bled, yet people seldom saw him sad.
His hands though 'quick' were skilled at carving toys for children of
    the street.
He was gentle where it mattered – like a hard soft-centred sweet.

Kiddo was an ideal person, when he stayed away from drink.
And he knew the danger clearly, for the likker made him think.
Think of how his life was going, and the pain that drove him wild.
There were days he spent in drinking, days he seldom ever smiled.

Till some guy who didn't know him, took a chance and called him
    out.
Kiddo relished in the conflict, as he smashed the man about.
Then next day remorse and sorrow made him lift the toys again.
And all the time his shoulders ached and tortured with the stinging
    pain.

Kiddo thought the pain he carried stemmed from humping sacks of
    flour,
Onto lorries, off the lorries. And the ache stayed hour by hour.
Sometimes as his weekday ended, tears would well within his eyes,
But he would wipe them with his cuff, and hurry home to his latest
    prize.

A fort he'd carved out for some youngster, sanded, polished with
    great care.
Never would the man complain, yet all the time the pain was there.
He'd sit and look his gnarled hands over, knuckles broken, fingers
    staved.
On one such finger was a ring, with his initials faint engraved.

He'd won that ring for beating Hanley, in the Chapel Fields one
    night,
Long ago when he was young, and fierce, and only lived to fight.
A guy once wrote about the Kiddo in the 'Ireland's 'Sar'day' Night'.
He still retained the yellowed cutting, which he'd read when he was
    'tight'.

He'd read it to the kids who loved him, 'Kiddo is,' he'd quote, 'Quite
    good.
And he didn't half belt Hanley. Mark my words, that Kiddo's
    shrewd.
He can punch, and he can take it. Never seen a guy as game.'
Then he'd crouch and play a punch. Yet all the time, the pain, the
    pain.

It got so bad, he saw a doctor, but the doctor shook his head,
Found no ailment, tut-tut-tutted. Kiddo, pain-wracked, took to bed.
He wasted like the snow in springtime; still the shoulder ached and
    stung
Till his anguished moans were heeded, and a hospital was rung.

The Specialist who operated said, 'That fellow's tough as nails,
But there's nothing that can help him, if this operation fails.
By the way, when he comes to, I hope you'll make him understand,
We couldn't wait to get consent. We had to amputate his hand.'

Gangarene had claimed some knuckles, though his shoulder gave the
    pain.
Kiddo's ache stemmed from that hand. The hand he'd never see
    again.
When he woke he smiled at Matron, said, 'By God, I'm feelin' gran'.
Not a twinge in my bad shoulder, just a stinging in my hand.'

Matron said his eyes turned frozen when he saw the bandaged
    stump,
And his face was agitated, like a fox that's caught by hunt.
Or a boxer who's been beaten, till his heart can take no more.
Kiddo groaned and rolled with anguish, rolled from bed and hit the
    floor.

'My hand; my bloody hand,' he whimpered, rolling like a storm-
   tossed boat.
'Why'd they cut my bloody hand off; should have cut my bloody
   throat.
How will Ellie get her dolls' house? Who will make a fort for John?
How can I dovetail or fret a piece of wood, my hand is gone.

The rocking horse that Jimmy wanted; who is gonna finish that?
That Doctor should have asked me first,' he sobbed whilst writhing
   on the mat.
The writhing tore his stitches open, letting blood flow dark and free.
'I can't fight, or finish toys off. . . Doc, oh Doc, you've murdered me.'

He saw the hand smash into Butler, watched it cut Mick Brady
   down.
Saw it tattoo Denver's features, felt it pulp the face of Brown.
Had it lifted beating Hanley. Had it broken facing Crump.
Now his mind's eyes glazed with horror, as he viewed the bandaged
   stump.

He saw it take a piece of timber, and with patience sand and plane.
Cut and cudgel, carve and whittle, till emerged a wooden train,
Or a fort, perhaps a garage. His throat constricted on a lump.
And he cried with uncocked fury, as he viewed the bandaged stump.

Kiddo's tear-stained face was ashen, as they put him back in bed.
Kiddo raved about the children as his torn stump bled and bled.
'Told wee Tom, I'd make a garage for to house his cars that shine.
Tell wee Tommy, won't you Matron, that the fault is yours not
   mine.'

Matron nodded quite serenely as she jabbed him full of dope.
Kiddo's eyes rolled in his head, he fought that drug without a hope,
Whilst his blood soaked the bed with a large dark stain,
And all the time, the pain, the pain.

They thought he'd lost the final round, but he survived and soon
   gained ground,
Because he learned that children stayed some distance from his now
   white bed.

22

And he just lived from day to day, to see the children and to play.
And though he couldn't make them toys, he kept them happy with
his noise.

And Matron even watched some nights, as Kiddo would re-live his
fights.
The kids would roar excitedly, as he tossed punches, one, two, three!
Then ducked a right only he had seen, and dropped an imaginary
Basher Greene.
And bathed in limelight full of joy, applauded by each girl and boy.

But then he heard of a child called Jim. The doctors held small hope
for him,
For if he slept, they swore it right, he'd never see the dawn's grey
light.
Jim was barely ten years old, and on him fever'd took a hold.
A fever they could lick all right, if they could get him through the
night.

But the lad was weak and small, and didn't seem to care at all.
Kiddo sneaked into his room, when night was throwing down its
gloom.
The boy was tired and drawn and pale; his eyes seemed covered by a
veil.
And he was just about to sleep, when in he saw the Kiddo leap.

'Hi Jim, I'm gonna show you now the way I beat ol' Gooze-Neck
Gow.
Of course it went near fifty rounds, for he out-weighed me twenty
pounds.'
Then with his mouth he made a 'ping', the way a ringside bell would
ring.
His bandaged stump flailed in the air, as he boxed a foe who wasn't
there!

But he fought with such intent, young Jim's eyes followed where he
went.
And Matron stood at the door and watched, and knew a plot was
being hatched,

23

As Kiddo danced and jabbed and hooked. And where he went young
   Jimmy looked,
With eyes that seemed to grow quite bright as Kiddo boxed on
   through the night.

He cast off coat and tie and shirt, then backed away like he'd been
   hurt.
Now and again, he grinned at Jim. Not seeing Matron watching him.
And Matron's eyes were full of tears, as Kiddo also cast off years,
And fought it out with Gooze-Neck Gow as though the fight was
   really now.

And seldom did he take a rest. His jabs and hooks were still the best,
Though perspiration rode his face, as round the makeshift ring he
   raced.
Matron jumped when he went down, but something made her stand
   her ground,
And she was glad, for she heard him say, 'See Jim, he caught me on
   the sway.

And dropped me when my guard was down, but I'll take a count then
   go to town.'
At that he rose and circled wide, 'He can run, young Jim, but he can't
   hide.
An' Jim,' he said, with gasping breath, 'It's just the same with life and
   death.
If you rise and show it fight, death will not beat you tonight.'

He tripped and fell, but raised a hand, 'Don't fret young Jim,' he
   gasped, 'I'm gran'.
Ol' Gooze-Neck's still got lots of guts, but he'll be mine — no ifs or
   buts.'
The Matron almost cried with shame, as Kiddo found his feet again.
And slowly shuffled, with guarded head, to fight a Gooze-Neck Gow
   long dead.

But the dawn's weak silver light was slowly winning out the night.
As Kiddo moved with legs of lead, and Jimmy sat up on the bed.

24

And yelled for Kiddo, fierce and shrill, and gave the old man strength
and will.
And although spent he swung the stump, I'm sure old Gooze-Neck
felt the thump.

And then the filtered rays of sun told him that the fight was won.
He said to Jim, 'I'm winner now, but give a cheer for Gooze-Neck
Gow.
It sure was a tough ol' bout, but now I've knocked him down and
out.'
And Matron's eyes were filled with joy, to see the change in that
young boy.

And though she'd stood there all night long, her heart was light and
full of song,
For life was now where life was not, all due to Kiddo tired and hot.
She thought a miracle, of love, had blossomed from the skies above,
And sent to them to aid the child, a man whose life was sad and wild.
A man whose heart went thump, thump, thump, as blood drained
from his bandaged stump.

And Kiddo never forgot that night. He stayed with Jimmy till the lad
was right.
And the fever waned till it finally went, as the moon goes when the
night is spent.
Now Kiddo sits at his front door, stump and shoulder never sore.
And tells the children with delight, of what he terms his 'greatest
fight'.
The night he knocked out Gooze-Neck Gow, and how big a man
young Jim is now.

Jack

Jack drank the last of his bitter brew,
   and gazed around the motley crew,
In donkey-jackets quaffing beer.
   His scornful smile turned to a sneer.
He listened to their pretty talk,
   and likened it to chicken-squawk.
He watched their faces work with drink,
   and heard their porter tumblers clink.
And knew he hated everyone,
   each mother's boy and father's son.
He spat with venom on the floor,
   and eyed the drinking men once more.

He eyed young Jimmy, boozing well,
   who now and then a yarn would tell,
Of knocking some girl up the pole,
   whilst Andy Black would curse his soul.
For Andy Black had daughters ten,
   he tried to keep from horny men.
But three had finished nursing kids,
   and near put Andy on the skids.
As was he drank for weeks on end,
   and cried because he couldn't fend.
He swore at Bell and said, 'You rats
   do everything but raise the brats,
You like to breed so bloody free,
   they're born and reared by mugs like me,
Who'd never show their girls the door
   but keep them even though they whore.'

His crabbit face was lined and grey,
   a man who'd seen a bitter day.
And people smirked behind their hand
   because he couldn't hold command
of daughters beautiful and gay.
   He lived in dread from day to day.

Jack's face lifted from the men
 and travelled round the pub again.
Filled by laughing, swearing souls,
 its heat was made by blazing coals.
Its ceiling was a dingy grey,
 its paintwork peeled and scraped away.
Its windows blocked from light of day,
 no wash for them from May till May.

He was jagged to life by a glassy clink,
 as Andy set him up a drink.
Jack glared at him, his face a mask,
 I want no drink; I didn't ask.
For in that bar it well was known,
 Jack Murphy liked to drink alone.
Sour. . . dogmatic in his beer,
 a villain with a built-in sneer.

'You bloody fool, what do you think?
 You think I'm in here bummin' drink!'
Old Andy cringed at this attack,
 in truth he was afraid of Jack.
As was each man, who drank inside
 that pub so near the Dock's black tide.
For Jack was heavy, wide and tall
 and harder than the bar's brick wall,
And meaner than a dog in pup,
 who maimed with pleasure when worked-up.

The sailor sprawling by the fire
 could testify to Big Jack's ire.
As could the docker drinking gin. . .
 for Jack had beat the hide off him.
The only crime for that attack was
 that he'd bandied words with Jack.
And Jack soured after a drink or two,
 and kicked the dockie black and blue.
The sailor too had learned his lesson,
 he crossed Big Jack, and fell like Nelson.

Billy Wilde who owned the 'house,
　　stood as quiet as a mouse.
And studied well the frightened men,
　　who muttered, 'Big Jack's off again.'
Or, 'God I'm glad I'm not the guy,
　　who's found ill favour in his eye.'
Or, 'Hope he doesn't hurt him much,
　　ol' Andy isn't bad as such.
He only tried to buy him ale. . .
　　I hope he lives to tell the tale.'

Fear was bright in Andy's eyes,
　　as vainly he apologised,
But Big Jack grabbed him by the throat,
　　and ripped the stitching in his coat.
And snarled, 'You lie – you bloody rat.'
　　He eyed the drink, 'You ordered that.
Don't try to say it's not for me,
　　you dirty stinking little flea.'

Young Jimmy Bell cried, 'Please don't, Jack,
　　you know oul' Andy can't fight back.
For Jesus' sake, a man like you
　　would break that poor oul fool in two.
He's sorry, Jack, he didn't think; we know
　　it's just your own you drink.'
'Shut up,' snarled Jack, 'or you I'll brain,'
　　and Jimmy didn't speak again.
And Jack retained his vice-like grip,
　　and then he snorted, 'Come Boy. . . sit. . .'
And Andy squatted like a dog,
　　and then Jack said, 'Croak like a frog.'
And Andy cried and croaked and sat.
　　While Jack roared, 'Now boys, what of that?'
But all the men felt small as flies,
　　for no man there was Big Jack's size.
So Jack continued on the track of
　　bullying old Andy Black.
He sneered at Andy, 'Guess you'll know

about the time I met your Flo.
You know, the one who isn't right,
   the one whose blue eyes shine so bright,
Who fills each pretty dress she wears
   with breasts that hang like young fresh pears.
She's kind of looney that may be,
   but boys, she seemed all right to me.
I saw her sunning in the park,
   and touched her face, just for a lark.
Her face was beautiful to see,
   the stupid bitch gave all to me.
So call me now a stinking rat,
   I took advantage of your brat.'

Old Andy blanched upon the floor,
   it seemed he couldn't take much more.
His face grew red, his lips were curled
   and filthy oaths at Jack he hurled.
'My simple Flo, I thought secure,
   from rats like you who make a whore,
Of girls who want no art or part,
   I'll have your black enamelled heart.'
And from his coat he drew a knife,
   and rushed at Jack to take his life.
The drinkers scattered from the scene,
   but Jack remained. His eyes were keen.
His knuckles caught the old man's head,
   and Andy fell like he was dead.
And sprawling on his open knife,
   he bled the last of his sad life.
Big Jack was neither shocked nor sad,
   he only said, 'Too bad, too bad.
He should have knowed I only joked him,
   still it wasn't me who croaked him.'
Judge said same but cautioned Jack,
   and stated he provoked attack.
And said , 'In duty I would fail,
   if I did not send you to jail.'
So three years' hard was Jack's reward,
   for helping Andy meet the Lord.

29

Jack had no kin, no friend to say,
  'I'll visit you on open day'.
He sat in woe, resigned to rot
  within the hated Prison-plot.
He cursed the warder, cursed the screw,
  and yelled, 'I'll torment all of you.'
He'd toss his food across the cell,
  and night by night he'd scream and yell.
At exercise, big man McKimm,
  took him aside and chastised him.
He said, 'It's sick the way you wail.
  (Big man was King-Pin in the jail)
You've copped a sentence which will stand,
  so try and face it like a man.'
Big Jack's left hand sunk in his gut,
  his right hand travelled half a fut.
McKimm woke up in Patch-Up Wing,
  and he remembered not a thing.
But at next exercise in 'yard',
  Big Jack was reckoned 'Prison-Hard'.
And he took over from McKimm,
  although the inmates hated him.

One day the warder shouted through
  the peep-hole, 'Visitor for you.
Stand to your door, I'll let you out,
  best promise not to scream and shout.'
The big man gasped, yet did agree,
  said, 'Who in God would visit me?'
He sat as quiet as a pup,
  until his visitor showed up.
He half-expected some old foe,
  but felt surprise when he saw Flo,
The same sweet Flo he'd met in Park.
  He nodded at the warder's bark:
'No kissing, touching, holding hands,
  just talking; that the Law commands.'
But lovely Flo was deaf and dumb,
  and from her lips no words would come.

Her fragile face was soft with smile,
    and threw Jack's mem'ry back a while,
To when he loved her in the Park.
    For once he felt compassion's spark –
Within a heart that waxed obscene,
    he thought he felt a pity wean.
She touched his hand and stroked it soft,
    the warder soared his eyes aloft.
But Big Jack couldn't understand,
    he'd killed her pa, she held his hand.

Although she couldn't say a word,
    a strange enchanting thing occurred.
A wistful smile of gentle grace
    shone from her eyes onto his face,
And drew the hate and fight from him,
    and made his past life fade and dim.
His hungry eyes ate at her form,
    and in his head the mem'ries swarm,
And yet the bad thoughts he won't think,
    and she to him becomes life's link.
And as the long years roll away,
    she visits him each open day.
And brings him cakes and holds his hands,
    and all the while he states his plans.
'Since you came here I've changed my tune,
    the warden says you've been a boon.
He hopes you'll always fill my booth,
    and so do I Flo, that's the truth.'

Sometimes he thought about that night,
    when she gave in without a fight.
To her, there was no right or wrong,
    Oh God, the mem'ry lingered long.
He'd savaged her to shame and pain,
    in Park with lust he'd been insane.
His love was savage, brutal, vile,
    yet sweet Flo never lost her smile.
'By God I've been a pig to you.

31

I wish to Him I could undo,
The wrong I did to you that day,
   Oh please forgive me Flo, I pray.
I love you girl, I'd give my arm,
   if I could just undo the harm
I did to you those years ago. . .
   Oh God, Oh God. . . Forgive me, Flo.'

He'd cry sometimes, just like a child,
   as sweet Flo held his hand and smiled.
The years went slowly by as Jack
   no more the warders did attack.
In fact he led a model life, and planned
   to make sweet Flo his wife.
And told the Guv'nor of his plan,
   and gained respect from screw and man.
And every open day came Flo,
   to smile at Jack who loved her so.

He dreamed of how his life would be,
   next year, when they would set him free.
He'd marry Flo and care for her,
   and never make life bare for her.
He'd get a job and mend his way,
   and love her more with every day.
The change in him was great they say.

Then came red-letter time for him,
   he shook the hand of Big McKimm,
And bid the Warden warm farewell —
   no more in prison would he dwell.
And Flo stood outside Prison gate,
   on that auspicious day and date,
Till Jack ducked through the little door,
   and held her in his arms once more.
But this time lust was not the cause,
   he loved her now for what she was.
A pretty orphant, kind and mild,
   a woman who was still a child.

32

He'd learned to talk to her with hands,
    and so they 'chatted' of their plans.
He held her tight and side by side
    they reached the pub close to the tide.

Flo entered first, then Jack came through,
    grinned broadly at the folk he knew.
He yelled, 'Don't fret, I'm turnin' nice
    and sweet. Flo's gonna be my wife.'
'Hush now!' his big harsh voice commands,
    'she's talkin' to me with her hands.'
They watched her spin the mental braille
    and saw his face turn shocked and pale.
And faster than the eye could note,
    her right hand flashed across his throat.
He thudded down like big tree felled.
    'She's cut his bloody throat!' they yelled.

Looking up, his eyes were pained,
    as from his neck the life blood drained.
It whooshed from vein like garden hose,
    and saturated sweet Flo's clothes.
He cried, 'Give me one last embrace.'
    She smiled and spat down on his face,
And with her eyes she drank the toast,
    that down in Hell his soul would roast.
And made it plain that daughters ten
    had someone to look after them.

They saw the knife that sliced his throat,
    was that which Andy brought from coat.
That day they picked him from the ground,
    the pocket knife could not be found.
Some said 'twas stole as souvenir,
    as police searched for it far and near.
And how it got in hands of Flo,
    was something only she could know.

33

Then Bill Wilde spoke, his voice cracked low.
    He rasped, 'I'm glad to see him go.
For all his life he's plagued my pub,
    a dirty rotten, ill-reared cub,
Who took from all and gave to none,
    except a broken neck or bone
With boot and fist and bloody head.
    Because of him her father's dead.'
He glared at those within his view
    and snarled, 'I'm warning each of you.
Jack Murphy's dead, and I'll swear free,
    that bloody thug was killed by me.'

For moments rare, a silence hung,
    then Docker said, 'Bill, hold yer tongue,
Shure any half-eyed fool could see –
    that imp of Hell was knifed by me.'
The knife was cleaned of fingerprint,
    and every man-jack did his stint.
'I stabbed the bastard,' Sailor cried,
    'although I'm sad the way he died.'
Young Jimmy yelled, 'Go swab the deck,
    you're tellin' lies, I killed Big Jack.'

When questions by the cop began,
    he got this story from each man.
'I killed the bastard, I croaked him.
    I made his light of life go dim.'
They yelled in unison at the cop,
    'I stuck the pig, I made him drop.'
And someone said, 'The others lie,
    for I'm the one who made Jack die.'
While someone from the back yelled, 'No!
    'twas me who laid the bully low.'
And all the raging hectic while,
    the woman never lost her smile.

Bill's clientele was brought en bloc,
    to stand indicted in the dock.

The judge said, 'It's beyond my ken,
   how can I hang so many men.'
The lawyer not one story broke,
   as each man claimed he made Jack croak.

The judge addressed the tragic lass,
   through learned hands his words were passed,
By mental braille which she knew so well.
   The judge's voice rang like a bell.
'With sympathy to you Miss Black,
   I'm sure you know who did attack,
The man you planned to wed quite soon,
   they tell me 'twas to be that noon.
Could you point out among this faction,
   the man who did this deadly action?'
Excitement in the courthouse piled,
   but sweet Flo only sat and smiled.

The judge could only end the case,
   he said with pity on his face,
'It's plain your heart's been torn apart,
   for life has been no apple cart.
He killed your dad, and done his time,
   now someone's added to the crime,
And killed the man you planned to wed.
   The only men you loved are dead.
You saddened girl, my heart goes out
   and to the villain I will shout.
He must be here among this crowd –
   Listen slayer, I hope you're proud!
This girl was wronged by the man who died,
   and wronged by everyone who lied.
She can't respond because of shock;
   someday she may and then I'll lock
The cur away until he hangs,
   or else goes mad with remorse pangs.'
His teeth were clenched as he angrily hissed,
   'Ad Nauseam. . . Case Dismissed!'

35

And sweet Flo wandered in the Park,
   and saw (but never heard) the lark.
She wandered smiling every day,
   until her golden hair turned grey.
They found her dead from heart attack,
   and scrawled in sand,
         'I loved you Jack!'

The ancient

for Davy Whiteside Senior

I know nought of his childhood, and less of his youth
But he's tarnished with principle, and drenched in the truth.
His face lined with thought spoke of knowledge supreme,
In the steely old eyes there still lurked a wild gleam,
The gleam in his eyes bared a heart full of wit,
And beneath the grey hairs was a brain I would pit
With the best of the Thinkers, whatever their fame,
For my good friend could match them at any old game.

We first met in the bar of a York Street saloon
Where some drunken old barfly was wailing a tune.
I by chance asked his views on the world as it stood;
His instant reply was, 'Youse kids have it good'.
He stepped back a pace, fixing me with a stare
(For a moment I wished that I hadn't been there!),
Emphasising the point with a thud of his hand,
He said, 'Son, tell me when youth has had it so grand.
As a boy I left school at the age of thirteen,
And was sent out to work, in the cold dark unseen.
Now you kids never have any holes in your pants
And if learning you lust, you can have college grants.

'In my day you were taught, sure enough, that is true,
But in fact what you learned was entirely up to you.
Now I'm old, mark you, seventy on the turn of next spring,
But I guess even now I could teach you a thing. . .
Every star in the sky I could mention its name
And I reckon that Hell never had any flame.
All my life I've gleaned wisdom, and stuck to details
And I'll try to learn more while this body prevails.'

He stopped, raised his pint glass and took a long draught,
And while he thus rested, I was tempted to ask
'Davy,' I said, with a long-drawn-out sigh
(His ears minched my words, as he formed a reply).

37

I quickly went on but he didn't intrude
For this gentleman scholar could never be rude,
'Davy,' I echoed, 'I'd study life through, just to sit on this
    bar stool
And match words with you!'

The Work

Slingin' cement on a hot summer's day
Was like an excursion to Hell, they say.
Blinded, melting, caked and tired,
One complaint and you'd get fired.

A day on the Quay

'Get down there,' he said to me. The man with stone for a face.
I went to say I'd rather not – he didn't stay to hear my case.
Stepping wisely, over hatch-boards, mind racing – what to do?
Who to team with? – all avoid me – no-one wants you, if you're new.

When the other four have teamed up, youth with cap and
    features tough,
Seems efficient, calls me to him. 'You and me,' his voice is gruff.
He spreads a sling, and beckons me to spread a sheet upon the deck.
That strip of canvas don't spread easy, when you haven't got
    the knack.

The knack you need to be efficient, like that big guy tough and
    strong.
He says, 'We'll "sink" pal, soft and easy.' God! the agony is long.
Pulling bags from locked positions, fingers gnawing tearing free.
Easy to my big strong friend, but such a torturous time for me.

When we'd cleaned that deep dark hatch and sent the sweepings to
    the shore.
I crawled up that long, long ladder; dusty, thirsty, aching sore.
All the dough I got that day. . . damned if it was worth the pain.
Fare thee well, old Belfast Docks, you will not see my face again!

Hell is the houl' of a Beg Boat

Hell is the houl' of a Beg Boat,
  slingin' out forty an hour
After a night on the likker
  when yer head an' yer belly's on fire.

You're dodgin' the 'heaves' that go flyin',
  whipped from the hatch to the shore;
Sweat's sweepin' down through yer eyebrows,
  you slip more than once to the floor;
Yer eye's on the hook as it travels,
  you don't want another sore head;
Yer hands grip the hard paper sackin';
  You're wishin' ye'd stayed in yer bed.
Yeah, Hell is the houl' of a Beg Boat,
  slingin' out forty an hour
After a night on the likker
  when yer head an' yer belly's on fire.

You look at yer mate as he labours,
  he's treatin' it all as a game.
All of his life he's teetotal –
  you're wishin' that you were the same!
The ganger is yellin' down at you,
  the winch block is screechin' for oil,
The shoremen are lappin' ropes round you,
  yer head feels like it's on the boil.
Yeah, Hell is the houl' of a Beg Boat,
  slingin' out forty an hour
After a night on the likker
  when yer head an' yer belly's on fire.

The winch hook comes swingin' in at you,
  you grab it and hook on yer 'heave';
The salt in yer sweat burns yer eyeballs,
  you wipe it away with yer sleeve;
You shout for a bucket of water,

the ganger looks down with a leer:
'I'll run down to Barnie's,' he chortles,
    'an' git you a nice pint of beer.'
Yeah, Hell is the houl' of a Beg Boat,
    slingin' out forty an hour
After a night on the likker
    when yer head an' yer belly's on fire.

Yer mate spreads the sling and the canvas
    an' tells you it's your turn to 'sink';
You claw at the sacks with yer fingers,
    Ye'd sell yer left leg for a drink.
The trick is to dig out the cargo
    with nothin' except yer bare hands.
You toss the first beg down behind you
    and choke in the dust as it lands.
Yeah, Hell is the houl' of a Beg Boat
    slingin' out forty an hour
After a night on the likker
    when yer head an' yer belly's on fire.

Ye're burrowin' just like a rabbit,
    tail over head in a bin;
You snarl for a bucket of water,
    the ganger just gives you a grin;
The sweepin' hook won't let you linger,
    you've got to keep sendin' out 'heaves':
You hook on, then start to another –
    you can't even watch as it leaves.
The paper sack's burnin' yer fingers,
    as down through the cargo you bore.
You're tossin' up begs to yer buddy
    an' prayin' you'll soon see the floor.
Yeah, Hell is the houl' of a Beg Boat,
    slingin' out forty an hour
After a night on the likker
    when yer head and yer belly's on fire.

Ye're haulin' and draggin' and stackin',
    until you at last see the floor.
Yer buddy drops in there beside you
    an' soon you make room for two more.
From then on the rest is plain sailin',
    you clear out the wings and the nose.
When the last ton is winched to the shore gang
    you heave a deep sigh as it goes.
Yeah, Hell is the houl' of a Beg Boat,
    Spewin' out forty an hour
After a night on the likker
    when yer head an' yer belly's on fire!

Little helper

Little helper, leave your shelter, jump into my searching hand.
Firmly nestle 'tween my fingers, snug your stock fits in my palm.
Let your one tooth seek the sackcloth, bury deep; I'll twist your head.
You give added strength to my arm (from the wound, no products
   bled).

Like a biting nimble puppy worry each sack to my reach.
Nipping, tipping, never ripping; just a tiny hole in each.
Draw those bags to the elevator, little finger made of steel.
Draw those sacks with prolonged fury. (You won't hurt the
   yellow meal.)

Just what would I do without you, flesh and bone cringe at the
   thought.
Fingers would get sore and blistered, if yourself I hadn't brought.
When the last bag has been lifted, and we're brushing up the dirt!
I make sure you nest securely (in the pocket of my shirt).

Tale of a Spud Boat

Monty and Devil and Smoke were ashore,
Closey and Lyttle and two or three more.
J.O. had the hook, with his back to the door.
    The day we loaded the *Caroline*.

Winkie and Wilsy and Joe in the houl',
Gibby was driving the winch with a scowl.
Scadger was puffin' because of the coul'.
    The day we loaded the *Caroline*.

The sailor said, 'We're for two hundred ton,
so up to the Cobblers I'll be able to run.
For it's gonna be late when youse are done. . .'
    The day we loaded the *Caroline*.

Nicholson showed us the spuds we'd to lift. . .
and so we proceeded the pile for to shift.
The winch was fast. . . the boat was a gift.
    The day we loaded the *Caroline*.

Majestics, King Edwards and 'Consuls' all were
stowed in the hatch with the greatest of care.
You load up the truck, then you run like a hare.
    The day we loaded the *Caroline*.

By noon the ship was ready for sea,
and gently moving away from the Quay.
A job well done, with that you'll agree.
    The day we loaded the *Caroline*.

The sailor came running out of the shed,
and managed to leap on the fo'c'sle head.
He shook his fist and his face was red.
    The day we loaded the *Caroline*.

He scowled at us as he sailed past,
and snarled, 'No men could work that fast.'
For his boots were still on the mender's last.
    The day we loaded the *Caroline*.

He said next time that he'd take note,
not to try and leave the boat.
In fact he wouldn't put on his coat.
    When next we load the *Caroline*.

'Casual' curses

Did you ever sign on the bloody 'Buroo', the bloody 'Buroo',
   the bloody 'Buroo',
You stand for hours in a big long queue
   In the bloody 'Buroo' in Belfast.
Did you ever sign on the 'Casual Box', the 'Casual Box',
   the 'Casual Box',
They say them lads take some sad knocks
   On the 'Casual Box' in Belfast.
They make you sign there every day, every day,
   every day,
And stop your dole if you go astray
   On the 'Casual Box' in Belfast.
Report for work at eight o'clock, eight o'clock,
   eight o'clock,
But there's no bloody work on the Belfast Dock,
   For the casual man in Belfast.
They'll starve yer kids on the word of a jerk, word of a jerk,
   word of a jerk,
Who'll swear ya didn't turn out for work
   On the 'Casual Box' in Belfast.
The way they look when they pay out your dockets, pay out
   your dockets, pay out your dockets,
You'd think it was out of their own bloody pockets.
   In the bloody 'Buroo' in Belfast.
I hope to God when my life is through, life is through,
   life is through,
Where I go they won't have any bloody 'Buroo'
   Like the bloody 'Buroo' in Belfast.

The tug-boat sailor

I was stannin' at the corner, when up came little Jim,
Says he, 'I'm lookin' for our kid, I've got a job for him.'
But Bouncer didn't want it, an' that's how I came to be
An O.S. on a tug-boat, the day I went to sea.

We made for Barnie Valerie's as all good seamen did
And lowered stout and Bannerman's (Jim subbed me half a quid).
Says he, 'It's time we motored, we're sailin' with the tide.'
I hurried through the dockgates, filled with Bannerman's and pride.

We headed for the Basin, where all the tug boats lay.
Arrivin' there quite breathless, we saw her sail away!
Says Jim, 'We'll catch her next time,' as we watched the sea gulls
    swarm;
'C'mon, a spot of shore leave wouldn't do you any harm.'

We headed back to Barnie's and drank Bannerman's and stout
In truth I didn't worry if the boat was in or out,
But Jim was made of sterner stuff, his life revolved in salt
So we staggered into Whitla Street and made the traffic halt.

Our ship was in the Basin. . . tied by head and heel.
The skipper eyed us from the bridge and watched us rock and reel.
Dressed like a civilian, a cloth cap adorned his head –
He looked at my limp figure and ordered me to bed.

When I woke the ship was tossin'; I felt sicker than a dog
For that night had all the mixtures of storm and rain and fog.
Wee Jim came down the ladder, his voice was warm and bright:
'I'm glad to see ye're shipshape, for we've got to work tonight.'

He helped me up the ladder, onto the open deck
The ship lurched in the weather – I had a sick attack!
I grimly hugged the boat rail, as my cargo spluttered out
And filled the scuppers ankle deep with Bannerman's and stout.

50

But wee Jim says, 'C'mon now, there's work we gotta do,
For this ship is a dry ship, except for me and you,
And though we love our likker we've got to make it plain
That we can do our duty, be it snow or hail or rain.

I did my duty that night. Although the squall howled high,
I stood my tug-boat station, and heeded every cry.
Though froze from bone to marrow, and drenched from head to toe,
I wouldn't leave my station, until Jimmy bade me go.

Well anyway, from that day, I never missed a tide,
And did my turn efficiently, with Jimmy at my side.
We worked hard on the high tide but whenever it went out
We sauntered down to Barnie's and drank Bannerman's and stout.

Casual conversation

What are ye havin' Bob. . . bottle an' a half un? what are ye at the
  day. . .?
Heysham, Mersey, Bristol, Clyde? God, ye're at the spuds, ye say.
How'd ye finish up at that, Bob?. . . Ach, ye say ye came in late. . .
Ach. . . it's better late than niver, an' sure a man cud have a worser
  fate
Than trundle spuds all bloody day. . . without a chance to get away;
  Or even git yer breath back!

Here's yer drink now. . . sup it up. . . I was at the Parcel Boat.
Finished now, free man again. Insurance cards are in me coat.
Wonder what there'll be tomorrow. . . someone says the Flour
  Boat's due.
Ach we'll haveta wait and see, Bob. . . nothin' else that we can do.

In the mornin'. . . standin', waitin', then the mad rush through that
  gate.
All the young 'uns, pushin', shovin', that's the bit I really hate.
Thanks a lot, I'll take a bottle. . . Aye, I'll have a wee one too.
'Member when we slung the 'Rosies'. Where's the big guy worked
  with you?
Strong as an ox he was, thon fella, good for a laugh and always
  funny.
God. . . I'm shocked to hear that, Bob. You say he's buried in
  Carnmoney.

Man, I'm really sad to hear that – Hi mate, givus another drink.
God, that guy was in his prime. And now he's dead. . . it makes you
  think.
Used to watch 'im in the houl'; he niver worried 'bout a thing.
The heaves he slung were straight and level. Stacked like soldiers in
  the sling.

Thirty-eight, ye say he was. . . five wee kids he's left behind.
It's sad to hear the big lad's buried. . . men like him are hard to find.

Heart, ye say. . . could have bin naught else. . . for sure that big guy
worked like Hell.
Used to watch 'im – strong – efficient. When yis slung the
'Oyster-Shell'.

Feel it now meself, sometimes. Dammit, Bob. . . we're gettin' oul'.
That work's hard enough for young 'uns. . . toiling in the blasted
coul'.
All them years of gettin' soaked; shirts turned black with rain and
sweat.
We should be home by the fire. . . all these years and no sense yet.

Ach. . . I wish I'd saved a few bob. So do you. . . we're both oul'
fools.
Only time we'll get some rest is when we win the bloody pools.
Aw. . . c'mon. we'll have another. Sentiment's a thing I hate.
Two more halfs. . . an' two more bottles. . . God. . . I'm sorry 'bout
your mate.

Belfast Dock

When I was young, I took to the road,
   that those who came before me strode. . .
I stood with the crowds in the cobbled pen,
   where the gangers schooled the casual men.
The work was tough, the conditions bad,
   and it didn't help to be a lad.
For the ganger's eyes would pierce and scan,
   as he probed the school for the 'all-round' man
Who could sling and stow, or drive a winch.
   With skills like these you'd be a cinch
To work each day in the ship or shed. . .
   but now it seems those times have fled. . .
Fork-lift truck and container box,
   you've torn the life from Belfast Dock.

Used to be you'd have toiled two weeks,
   in a timber boat, using long sharp cleeks.
Working night and day till the holds were clear,
   sweating under the ganger's sneer.
Whilst splinters cut your hands to pieces;
   the jibing foreman never ceases,
As he goads you on to perfect his plan,
   to mould another 'all-round' man.
One he can use or discard at whim,
   for you're just a face in the crowd to him.
But your painful learnin' when you were young,
   has come to naught, now the wood's pre-slung.
Palletised timber in four-ton block,
   you've torn the life from Belfast Dock.

Livestock travel in mobile pens,
   from Irish farms to Scottish glens,
They reach their destination quick,
   without a tap from a docker's stick.
And yet it isn't so long ago,
   when dockers travelled to and fro.

I still can hear the baleful bleats
  of beasts being herded through narrow streets.
Where we as kids would help bring back
  those which ran off from the pack,
Frightened creatures from a steaming herd
  in Prince's Dock Street, runnin' scared.
But mobile pens and crated livestock,
  you've torn the life from Belfast Dock.

Now I muse as I watch the scenes
  of ships unloaded by huge machines,
stripping hatches in record time,
  sometimes progress can be a crime.
More work done by fewer men;
  most are left in the schooling pen.
Mechanical shovels scooping 'bulk' –
  it's enough to make a 'bag-man' sulk!
For 'Bag Boats' used to be ten-a-penny. . .
  now you'll find there's hardly any,
As these giant monsters clear the quay
  quick as you'd drink a cup of tea.
Dieselled horses working round the clock,
  you've torn the life from Belfast Dock.

Empty berths and cranes awastin',
  flattened sheds and tarmac'd basin.
Forktruck. . . shovel. . . 'bulk' and block. . .
  you've torn the life from Belfast Dock!

The Fights

It's said aggression in their hearts
    was difficult to smother,
And if a stranger wouldn't fight
    they'd set upon each other.
But malice never reigned too long.
    They'd meet to slake their thirst,
And try to figure out the bout
    and who hit who the first.

To be a fightin' man

To be a fightin' man, you've gotta know
      Which guy's fast, and which guy's slow.
      Which guy's muscle, and which guy's fat.
      Which guy's easy, and which guy's not.
      Which guy's wind is gonna last.
      Which guy's better days are past.
      Which guy's gonna make you work.
      Which guy's just a loud-mouthed jerk.
      Which guy packs a heavy punch.
      Which guy's tough when with a 'bunch'.
      Which guy doesn't wanna know.
      Which guy's gonna make you go.
      Which guy's got a dirty streak.
      Which guy's mean, and which guy's meek.

To be a fightin' man ye've gotta face
      Brawling at a hectic pace.
      Crawling in a public place.
      Mauling someone else's face.
      Falling into much disgrace.
      Going sober to finish a fight
      You started whilst drunk on the previous night.
      Nerves raw, and head sore,
      From punches taken the night before.
      Ready, even willing to die,
      Just to prove you're a better guy.

If these things you can withstand,
      You're near enough a fightin' man.
      But before you rush to start,
      You're not worth a damn
      If you haven't got heart.

Fightin' talk

I could left hook you over the table,
 But that wouldn't prove any point.
I could slay you like Cain did with Abel,
 But that would just break up the joint.
So I'll give you ten seconds to leave here,
 And hope that you'll take my advice,
'Cause I'm kinda liberal with talkin',
 And I don't boil my cabbages twice.

You're young, and you're tough and you're stubborn;
 You want me because I'm the best.
You've beaten the others who faced you;
 You think I'll fold just like the rest.
Well, maybe you're right, I've grown older,
 My breathing is not what it was,
But I'll beat rings 'round any of you punks,
 'Cause I fight with my brains not my jaws.

So if you remain here to face me,
 I'll show you how veterans fight.
I'll gouge out your eyes, and I'll boot you,
 I'll knee you, and butt you and bite.
I'll break both your arms, and I'll choke you,
 I'll bite the ears clean off your head.
I'll kick in your teeth, pull your hair out.
 You'll wake up in a hospital bed.

So take yourself off by the hand boy,
 You've got some inches to grow
Before you can mix it with me son –
 And don't slam the door as you go!

An enlightened frightened fightin' man

I fight with my fists and my boots, and my head.
    I fight 'cause I don't like to run.
I've belted with zest 'cause I'm poor and oppressed
    but I don't want to fight with a gun.
A kick in the thigh, or a punch in the eye
    is nothing compared with the feel
Of a bayonet tearing its way through your ribs,
    or a lung that's been punctured by steel.

A personal hate fired by rage can create
    a reason for combat to start,
And the fire in your eyes, for a face you despise
    lights a fuse that's attached to your hearts.
Then your fists start to fly, as you pummel the guy
    with a venom that you really mean,
But how can you boot at, never mind shoot at,
    a fellow that you've never seen.

I'll say it again, I know fighting's insane,
    and not to be treated as fun,
But I'll still take a chance with a jab and a dance –
    I ain't gonna fight with a gun.

A guy I know

There's a venom in that fellow, but he keeps it bottled tight
Until somebody needles him, and forces him to fight.

There's a savage in that fellow, but it lies beneath the skin,
And only shows its presence when someone angers him.

There is courage in that fellow. And it's there for all to see.
He wears it on his proud face, and his foes don't disagree.

There's compassion in that fellow; but he seldom lets it show,
For sadness is a quality no fighting man should know.

There is sorrow in that fellow, and he keeps it in his eyes.
He hates to hurt his fellow man.
    And afterwards,
              He cries.

Thumb-nail sketch of a bar-room brawl

There was five to two, in the bar-room brawl –
    when one of the five reeled back,
From a fierce and frantic onslaught, that began
    the main attack.
His assailant, in a light blue shirt, then turned
    and snarled out loud:
'Though you be more, by God I'm sure, you'll find
    we won't be cowed.'
The one who suffered from his fist wiped
    his mouth to say,
'Before we're finished with youse guys, you won't
    forget this day.'
His hate-filled eyes cruised 'round the room;
    'Listen all,' he said.
'Anyone who aids these bums is gonna wind-up dead.'

The five charged in a wild melee, two men
    went down; it was two to three.
Though Blue-shirt fought relentlessly, his pal
    went down. It was one to three.
He faced his foes; and squared his feet.
    The toughest guy they'd ever meet.
I think they kinda knew it too. They'd bitten
    off. . . but they couldn't chew!
Blue-shirt leapt and threw a hook, his hard
    fist crunched on bone.
He swung again, one writhed in pain, and to
    the floor was thrown.
His face was cut below one eye, and blood
    poured down his cheek.
He stood triumphant and unbowed, like some
    huge warring Greek!

Again he pounced with hands and feet and dropped
    another one.
And then they both stood face to face, they
    who had begun.

The one who threatened Blue-shirt would not
    forget the day,
Was gonna find to his surprise, it would not
    end that way.
They eyed each other warily, a knife flashed
    in the light.
Blue-shirt leapt and kicked it high, by God
    that guy could fight.
With boot and fist, he seldom missed, and
    brought the cur to bay.
Then hoisted up his fallen friend. . .
    and quickly walked away!

Suckered again

'If I'd bin thirty when he was thirty,
  I'd have tried him and not felt so dirty;
But now he's kinda lost his sting.
  And to beat him now wouldn't mean a thing.'
So said Dandy McIntyre, sitting at the pub's
  big fire.
Drinking pints 'cause they were free, bought by
  mugs like you and me.
Who always like to hear the crack; when fightin'
  men their fights enact.

'Once I felled big Jimmy Jones. I nearly busted
  all his bones.
With one great blow, which, I swear to all, if I'd
  missed would've carried me through the wall.'
'We all know it's not strength you lack,' a little
  voice piped from the back.
'And though your talk's all guts and fire, you don't
  fool me, Big McIntyre.
You couldn't beat big Jim McKee, if you were thirty
  and he was three.'

Dandy's face got very red. 'Listen squirt – it's
  like I said,
McKee's past thirty, and lost his sting. And to
  beat him now wouldn't mean a thing.'
'Ack. . . talk is chape,' said the little man,
  'but now I'm gonna force your hand.
A fiver each Mac. . . that's the call. Big Jim
  and you. . . and winner take all!'
'Man, that sounds great. . . I'd love a fight. . .
  but sure I haven't got a light.'

'Now Mac. . . a fightin' man like you should
  have his backers. . . like we do.
And if you can't back up your talk, then you
  know you shouldn't squawk!'

Dandy's face was rather grey, as the pip-squeak
    walked away.
Just then I had a winning notion. 'Hold it –
    I'll put forth a motion. . .
Among us here we'll raise the dough, if to
    the fight you'll let us go.'

Both men gave us their consent, and so we
    gathered up the 'rent'.
And went to watch 'em in a field. . . to see
    who'd be the first to yield.
Dandy McIntyre looked great; Jim McKee seemed
    underweight.
When the betting had begun, Jim McKee was three
    to one.
We shovelled dough on McIntyre – 'cos he
    showed the pep and fire.

The little squirt took every bet, said our
    notes would all be met.
Anyway, they squared around, then McIntyre was
    on the ground.
Grovelling from a mighty punch, and clutching
    where he put his lunch.
When he didn't rise again, I saw our dough go
    down the drain.
Jim McKee had 'scooped the pool', man I felt
    an awful fool.

Now I know how that saying started, about 'a
    fool and his money, soon being parted.'
'Cos I'm sure the punch that 'felled' the 'hard',
    missed him by a 'half a yard'.
And it didn't do much harm. . . 'cause them three
    walked off arm in arm.
And while we're left with only pence. . .
    they're drinking scotch at our expense.

Jab and move

Jab and move it. Jab and move it. There is something you must prove.
Jab and move it, you must prove it. Throw that left out. Jab and
  move.
He's a fighter, and you're lighter, whilst he's tough as rusty nails.
So don't chance it. Jab and dance it. Float it, while his strength
  prevails.

He's a heavy and the levy of his punch could wear you down.
Jab and wing him, float and sting him. Keep your cool. . . or else
  you'll drown. . .
Drown beneath a storm of punches that will rock you to the core.
His body feels it as you weal it. Raw and red, and splotched and sore.

So jab and move it, you can prove it. Brain can often master might.
You can prove it. Jab and cruise it. Left, left, left. Hold high your
  right.
See his face-flesh split and curdle, see his eyes turn black with blood.
Keep the right up, and the spite up. Move. . . and he'll punch you
  where you stood.

Now his mouth is wide and gaping. Jab and move it, now's the proof.
Brain can often beat the brawler. Make that left sing: 'Bouf-Bouf.
  Bouf.'
Now his eyes are blank, unseeing. Cross your right-hand fast and
  slick.
Watch him topple, like an apple, reach that neutral corner quick.

See the ref droll out the seconds, see him strive to gain his feet.
Leap in triumph. He won't make it, and he grovels in defeat.
Now the ref will raise your gloved hand, as again you grin and leap.
Leap one more rung up the ladder. Boy! You jab and move so sweet!

Sound sense

I stopped punchin', and started talkin',
   the day my bones got sore
From 'shipping' too many right-hooks,
   and sprawling to the floor.
When you get old and slow down,
   it ain't the thing to fight.
Especially when you've lost the power
   to reason wrong from right.

For weakened men seek weaker prey,
   it salves their fading pride.
And keeps them on the Carousel
   that only youth can ride.
You're ornery and you're stubborn,
   yet lack the strength of arms
To cheat, defeat an enemy.
   They seem to come in swarms.

They make you fight for nothing.
   They force your hand with glee.
In better days those lowly curs
   would not have mixed with me.
But I played ends against the middle;
   let myself grow tight and fat,

Shipped the punches, took the crunches –
   Life gets tough when it's like that.
So now I talk to young 'uns,
   'cause I just ain't got the pace.
To meet them in a stand-up
   that would surely change my face.

A lesson learned the hard way

Fight if you're needled, pal, fight if you're stung.
Fight if you're elderly, fight if you're young.
Fight if you're tempted to, fight if you're scared.
Fight if you're picked upon, fight if you're dared.

Fight if you're cheated, son, fight if you're scorned.
Fight if you're threatened, fight if you're warned.
Fight if you're spat upon, fight if you're sad.
Fight if you're faulted, fight if you're mad.

Fight if you're cornered, boy, fight if you're not.
Fight if your blood's boiling, fight if you're fat.
Fight for your livelihood, fight any punk.
But never, no never friend, fight when you're drunk.

The Troubles

'I'm sorry for your troubles,' said the
   Catholic to the Prod.
'Aye,' replied his counterpart.
   'It's just the work of God,
Someday He may tell us, when our
   life is done. . .
Why we shot your brother
   and why youse killed my son.'

The dark bad days

The dark bad days are here again,
Once more the bards will lay acclaim
To men who take the lives of men.
The dark bad days are here again.

Insidious peace will not prevail,
While reforms crawl like a bloated snail,
And men are whipped by passion's flame.
The dark bad days are here again.

The spoken word can culminate,
Permeate a frenzy black with hate,
And slip the leash of death and pain.
The dark bad days are here again.

If again the bullets sing,
Who will gain from this sad thing?
Words just hurt, but bullets maim.
The dark bad days are here again.

When the blood of man has bled,
When we crawl forth to count the dead,
Will they all have died in vain?
The dark bad days are here again.

November 1968

Freedom fighter

What do you see when you dream, Freedom Fighter,
What do you see when you dream?
Do the corpes walk, do the mutilated scream?
What do you see when you dream?

What do you see in the gloom, Freedom Fighter,
What do you see in the gloom?
Do the spectres lurk in the corner of your room?
What do you see in the gloom?

What do you think when you sing, Freedom Fighter,
What do you think when you sing?
Do you think what you did was a glorious thing?
What do you think when you sing?

What will you do when you die, Freedom Fighter,
What will you do when you die?
When they take your gun and there's nowhere to run?
What will you do when you die?

What does it matter?

What does it matter what puts you out,
The bomb or the gun or the legalised shout,
The UVF or the IRA,
The men who burn or the men who pray,
The Hibernian Lodge or the Orange Band,
The bailiff or the Lords of the land,
The racketeer or the hate-filled note
That the neighbour inflamed with insanity wrote,
The merchants of death with their feathers and tar,
The sinister men in their weapon-filled car,
The fellow who draws at a map of the town
Red-lining the houses he wants to knock down,
Who couldn't care less if you end in a ditch,
So long as his new ring road runs without hitch;
The gifted orators who fashion the hate
That spews from the fitter or plumber or mate,
Who fan it with porter and then heave a stone
At the home of some old one who lives all alone?
What does it matter what puts you out,
Be it progress, injustice or small-minded lout,
Or the midnight marauder whose bigoted shriek
Sends terror to bed with the aged and weak?
What does it matter what put you out,
When you're old or alone and just can't get about,
And you're plucked from your roots like an unwanted weed.
What does it matter whose hand did the deed?

March 1971

Belfast 69–76

Belfast is a sullen town, spawned upon a stream,
  born to cries of murder, and midwifed by a scream.
Belfast is a bleak town, with dark and dull mean streets,
  where man greets with suspicion every stranger that he meets.

Belfast is a sad town, its moods are deep and black.
  sometimes it fights to shake the mites of hatred from its back. . .
Belfast has been martyred by men who love it dear
  and Belfast has been bartered by men who hide a sneer.

Belfast has been pummelled by men who find it fun
  to beat it into debris with bomb, grenade and gun.
Belfast is a sullen town, spawned upon a stream,
  born to cries of murder, and midwifed by a scream.

Sing a song of York Street

Sing a song of York Street, take me back again
To Big Davey and Buck Alec as they brawl in Stable Lane;
With doffers screamin' round 'em, they fought a brutal bout
Wearin' only trousers, with their bellies hangin' out.

Tell me 'bout the chancers, the hard-chaws and the brass;
Sing a song about the days that all too soon have passed.
The square setts and the pavers and the gas lamps have all gone;
The characters have vanished, but the memories linger on.

Tell me 'bout the pawnshops, where yis went when times were bleak
And pledged the oul' lad's Sunday suit to see yis through the week.
Tell me more of Rinty, an' how he won his crown
On that night yis lit a 'boney' that was seen all over town.

Heagan's home-baked sodas; Wilson's boiled pigs' feet;
Barnie Conway's Guinness; Fenton's finest meat;
Buttermilk from Turner's; Geordie's fresh ice-cream;
The Queen's and Joe McKibben's – all have vanished like a dream.

Sometimes I go down there an' sorta make the rounds.
I see them in my mind's eye, and hear their phantom sounds;
I hear the tumblers clinking, and see the faces plain.
Please sing a song of York Street and take me back again.

Acknowledgements

Some of these poems have previously been broadcast on BBC Radio
Ulster or published in the following:
*Belfast Telegraph, Sunday News, Worklines: Belfast Working Class
Poetry 1930–67* (Eye Publications).

The Publishers would like to thank the Mathildenhöhe Darmstadt
and Margaret and Gerry Grant of Newcastle (who own the cover
painting) for their kind and invaluable help.